Blockchain

I0005241

THE DATABASE REVOLUTION THAT WILL

CHANGE THE WORLD

By Jake Whiteley

By Jake Whiteley

Introduction

Congratulations on downloading *Blockchain: The Database Revolution That Will Change the World!* And thank you for doing so.

While blockchain is still such a relatively new technology that its true potential has not yet been ascertained, that hasn't stopped analysts from all sectors from jumping on it ravenously and declaring it the most important technology since the internet itself. Despite the fact that if you are not familiar with blockchain then these claims sound quite farfetched, the short answer is that yes, blockchain is likely going to change the world in your lifetime, it just isn't quite there yet.

With this unavoidable future in mind, it then becomes clear that learning everything you can about blockchain now, will better prepare you for a future in which it has caught on in the mainstream. As such, the following chapters will discuss everything you need to know in order to understand just what all the fuss is about when it comes to blockchain, starting with a breakdown of just what the word means and why it means different things to different people. After learning about the history of blockchain and some of its most common uses, you will then learn many of the ways that it has yet to reach perfection and the mistakes that are often made when implementing it for the first time, lest you expect it to solve your every problem. Finally, you will learn how to determine if a blockchain decentralized database is really worth all the extra effort and cost that will go into setting up and how to go about taking advantage of your own blockchain.

There are plenty of books on this subject on the market, thanks again for choosing this one! Every effort was made to ensure it is full of as much useful information as possible, please enjoy!

Chapter 1: Blockchain Explained

If you have heard the phrase blockchain thrown around in one context or another but still aren't quite sure just what is being discussed exactly, don't feel bad you are certainly not alone. The truth of the matter is that despite the fact that it has been around for less than a decade the phrase blockchain already means different things to different people. Currently, when a person is talking about blockchain, odds are they are talking about it in relation to crypto currencies in general or possibly in connection with bitcoin specifically as this was where the technology got its start. Additionally, these days you will likely hear the phrase in conjunction with that of smart contracts on an increasingly regular basis.

While the usage, and certainly the correct usage, will vary, there are a few things that any discussion of blockchain are likely to have in common. First and foremost, blockchains can be used to store data, primarily financial transactions though this is not required, in an extremely decentralized manner. Each new block of the chain then contains all the data of the previous blocks as well as the new information that will then be added, not just to the current block, but retroactively to all the other blocks as well.

In addition to all of the details in the chain and its own new details, each block then also contain a timestamp that catalogs when it was accessed as well as helping to define its place in the overall chain. This, combined with its automatically replicating nature means that it is able to work properly without the help of any type of central authority or server telling it what to do, potentially across thousands and thousands of individual data nodes located all around the world. These nodes then communicate with one another to obtain a group consensus when it comes to the validity or specific points of data.

Regardless of their purpose, all blockchains are going to have two primary types of users, those who have read only access and those that have write access as well. While access to more centralized databases must be tightly controlled, the very nature of the blockchain makes changing the data held within an extremely costly proposition. The specifics of blockchain security are discussed in detail in a later chapter.

Bitcoin beginnings

For those in the know, the writing is on the wall and it points to blockchain being one of the most influential technologies of the twenty-first century. Like all great innovations, it had humble beginnings, however, specifically as a theory floating around on a peer-to-peer programming message board by someone, or a group of some ones, using the false name of Satoshi Nakamoto.

Nakamoto first put forth the theory behind what would become blockchain as a way to create reliable peer-to-peer transactions without having to deal with any type of financial institution as an intermediary.

From this first theoretical consideration, the idea soon blossomed into a treatise on the topic entitled *bitcoin: A P2P Electronic Cash System* along with the original code for bitcoin that was released in an open source state as a proof of concept for the process. With the source code now out in the open, several new developers began working on the project in earnest and Satoshi Nakamoto was never heard from again after the spring of 2010.

To fully understand blockchain, a bit more of a discussion of bitcoin is warranted, as one would not exist without the other.

Bitcoin is a type of currency that exists solely online outside of all of the traditional checks and balances associated with world currencies.

In practice, those who use bitcoins these days are going about their business in a standard fashion, trading bitcoins in exchange for goods and services to retailers who accept the currency, in much the same way that online mainstay PayPal offers checking account-like services to its customers.

Where blockchain comes in is related to the way in which these transactions are then recorded and subsequently tracked in the long term. What this means is that if you go out and download the required files to start your own bitcoin node, part of what you are downloading is every transaction that has ever taken place through the bitcoin service. Specifically, when a new transaction occurs it is checked for accuracy and authenticity using a system that a person referred to as a bitcoin miner has created for just such a purpose. This bitcoin miner then uses that system to verify the information in the block that was created to house the transaction in question logically lines up with all of the data from the preceding blocks in the chain. To compensate them for the effort, bitcoin miners are then paid a percentage of a single bitcoin for their work. This process of unbiased third party verification is a key component of what makes a decentralized database possible.

While only receiving a small portion of a single bitcoin might not sound like much for running a system dedicated to helping keep a fully functioning economy afloat, at the end of 2016 a single bitcoin was worth just shy of $900, having experienced a nearly $300 increase in value between August and December of that year. The value of each individual bitcoin is related to the value of all the other coins on the market as well as the global exchange as a whole, just like more traditional currencies.

Also like other currencies, it is vulnerable to supply and demand which can affect its price both positively and negatively. The Nakamoto alias was the first user to mine bitcoins after he gifted 50 bitcoins to another user, creating the first block of the world's first blockchain in the process. The first recorded instance of someone using bitcoins to purchase real world products occurred when someone used 10,000 bitcoins to purchase $20 worth of pizza, setting the original price of a bitcoin at around .002 cents. To put that into perspective, at the time of writing this, 10,000 bitcoins are worth close to $9 million. I hope the pizza was good!

After its creation, the code that powered bitcoin, and thus blockchain, continued to be improved upon. This led to an important advancement in 2014 whereby a process was discovered that allowed entire programs to be inserted into individual blocks, creating the possibility for the first smart contracts to be crated and also the addition of data that was not strictly financial in nature as well. A smart contract is essentially a program that is capable of triggering once a specific if/then statement that occurs within the blockchain takes place to move funds from one place to another.

2016 marked another important year for blockchain technology as another type of crypto currency, this one known as Ethereum, made its way into the public consciousness in a bigger way. It is uniquely important to the ongoing development of blockchain software for its modifications to the way that users can create smart contracts making this process easier than ever to complete, leading many to call its code the basis for blockchain 2.0. This was followed by the Russian Federation's announcement that it was looking into a blockchain solution for the issues it has with copyright infringement which makes Russia the first nation to consider using blockchain on a major scale.

Centralized versus decentralized databases

When it comes to utilizing a blockchain for database purposes the biggest difference between it and a more traditional type of database is where the data is physically stored.

When it comes to traditional databases, various data servers and related nodes might be split up throughout a building, or even a few square miles, but, as a general rule, physical distance is minimized as much as possible to improve the speed with which the data can be accessed from various predetermined points.

On the other hand, blockchain nodes can be literally anywhere which means that dealing with latency is going to be a given no matter what. While this may not be ideal if you are looking to access large amounts of data in an extremely short period of time, if you are looking for a way to store information outside of the confines of any one location that ensures that many people can access it but not tamper with it, there is no better option than blockchain. This is the root of what makes blockchain such a potentially disruptive technology as it could alter the way the entire financial industry handles their data. Put simply, blockchain has the potential to revolutionize currency transaction in the way that the Internet affected the transference of information.

Chapter 2: Parts of a Blockchain

Resilient cryptography: While the fact that individual segments of a blockchain can replicate themselves into new nodes is novel from a technological perspective, it wouldn't be worth much of anything if the data that it held wasn't easy to see but difficult to get to without the proper authorization. This means that it is very easy to give users read only access without worrying about those users then using that to gain write access. What's more, the facet of the blockchain that ensures its security remains on point isn't some code specifically written for the task that can then be bypassed, the security comes from its very nature.

Because a blockchain is decentralized to its very core, it needs a reliable way to ensure that the information that is being disseminated remains the same across all the various nodes that make up a particular network. To do this, it simply checks the new data against all of the existing data and if more than 50 percent of the nodes support the information in question then it is changed across all the relevant nodes.

As such, if someone wanted to utilize fraud on a blockchain network, say by using the same bitcoins to make two different transactions, they would need to generate enough false transactions that showed that the coins were not used the first time to ensure that 51 percent of the total transactions showed the false details as opposed to the truth. This type of endeavor would be extremely cost prohibitive and require obscene amounts of energy, essentially making it more trouble than it is worth.

Best travel model: Blockchain information comes in two types; the transaction data and the information that surrounds it which helps the chain as a whole determine where individual blocks are supposed to fall into place. The transaction data makes takes up the majority of the space and it is passed along via what is known as a best-effort model which means it moves throughout the network based on which nodes would be easiest for it to move to next so it doesn't require a guiding hand of any type. When new data is found it is verified to be accurate before a block is created around it, which is where the third party verification and compensation model comes into play.

Private and public options*:* While one of the nice things about using blockchain for financial transactions is that anyone can see in without necessarily being able to interact with the data, when a new blockchain is created it is possible to ensure it is only visible to a limited number of people. Public blockchains are always going to have higher costs than the private alternatives because they have to be significantly more complicated in order to prevent fraud. Additionally, steps will need to be taken to ensure that each transaction is accurately validated to retain some semblance of overall order as well. Private blockchains don't need to worry about these types of costs because every person who has access to the chain can be in charge of validating transactions for the benefit of the group as a whole.

Returning to bitcoin once again, if a person is interested in setting up a bitcoin node then they first are required to download what is known as the Bitcoin Core which is required if they plan on verifying the transactions of others. The process of verifying these transactions will then create new blocks to add to the chain, which then must be, verified themselves across a majority of the network before they are added to the chain officially. On the contrary, in a private blockchain individuals are given clearance to access the blockchain in the first place so secondary security measures are left up to the creator's discretion.

Proof of work: When a new transaction is added to a node it is then verified based on all the other transactions in the node in question before being added to official timeline. Once this is done the chain inherently knows where the transaction data falls in the log and files it properly without the need for a guiding hand. Beyond this, each block also contains what is known as a proof of work system, which lets the chain know that it was created by the chain and not by an outside source. This proof of work requires a fair amount of computational power to complete and scales based on the number of required transactions, leading to the previously mentioned difficulty of getting enough power together to pull off blockchain based fraud.

Hashes: The security present in each blockchain is multifaceted which means that even if someone managed to gain access to the data contained in a blockchain they wouldn't immediately see all of the recorded transactions and would instead see what is known as a fixed length output which is essentially the unique fingerprint for the data in question meaning that even changing a single digit will lead to unpredictable results. The most commonly used hash function is SHA-256 and it takes the data provided and formats in such a way that only the same hash can then decode it and make it usable in the traditional sense.

Each block is given its own hash at the moment it is verified and added to the chain. The basic hash is then modified even further with additional details relating to the block's location in the chain and the relation the block's data has to the data in the surrounding blocks. If the details related to a specific hash don't match up with what a new node is expecting, then the block is denied.

Autonomous as it needs to be*:* The decentralized nature of the blockchain means that each node is able to operate as autonomously as possible for as long as possible. When it does finally come back in touch with the rest of the network then all of the other nodes will be able to seamlessly update their information without missing a beat. What's more, when this occurs the nodes that are closest to the returning node are leaned on more heavily as their connection to the new data naturally meets the best-effort definition as well. A final check then ensures that the new information contains nothing that is duplicate or conflicting with the rest of the chain before the new data is accepted and disseminated.

Merkle trees: Merkle trees are an important part of a blockchain's data storage process. Even though it is possible for the blockchain to be built without one, those that are created in this way are not as easily accessible for any parties involved nor are they as efficient overall. As previously discussed, each block within the blockchain has multiple transactions stored inside. Each transaction is put through a hash function and assigned its own unique hash as a result. The pairs of hashes are combined and then put through another hash function causing even more unique hashes to be made from this process.

The hashes combine in pairs to create more hashes until a singular unique hash is left from the rest. The completed result is called a root hash, which completes the Merkle tree or chain, this chain can be thought of as the sum total of all the various hashes that are a part of it. The Merkle chain is used to secure the blockchain and alert it of any changes with any of the hashes. Each hash goes through the process of being checked to make sure it matches the original hash every single time a new node is added.

Merkle trees make it possible to run the decentralized node structure that gives blockchain much of its mutability. They are a matrix of functionality and efficiency, a utilization of complexity and finesse. Merkle trees allow finances to be compacted into information that allow users to process the flow of trade with ease, even when they trade overseas.

The Merkle tree usually has branches that split off in factors of two. This means that each node has at least two things that branch off of it as a means of evenly distributing data verification. They can also be used to encode many files that happen to be smaller than the original file itself.

Just like in many other peer-to-peer network systems the data verification nature of Merkle trees has become a crucial part of the way things function as it allows the same pieces of information to exist in multiple places at the same time without risking a corruption of the entire chain, should that data suddenly no longer agree. If a piece of the data happens to be changed then it needs to be changed in a majority of the locations the entire chain exists in before the chain as a whole will except it as fact. It is very time consuming to go through and check all of the information manually so this is where Merkle trees come into play. They help limit the amount of information that has to be shared over the breadth of relevant nodes and make it easier for each node to find and verify disparate nodes to create a reliable picture of what the accurate details should be.

Every time a hash has found a match it is flagged before the next level of branches is checked to make sure that they all happen to match up as a way of determining the extent of disparity. This allows the process to happen much more quickly than if all of the data in question was being checked at each node, a must when the distance between nodes is potentially vast. Thanks to the hash and Merkle tree systems there is no reason to check the whole file as long as the individual hashes all matches up to one another.

A lot of the Merkle tree's system relies on trust, specifically the trust of the user in the sanctity and viability of the blockchain. When the user decides to create a node and download the chain the most recent version can be easily checked before the download begins to ensure the proper version of the blockchain is transmitted. This is the reason that it is called a Merkle tree because it's systems work like a bundle of growing branches from the roots of a tree. Any nodes that have been picked up from sources that are not trusted are checked against the true original hash. Once they have been checked and approved, the progress soon continues to download. If the information provided by multiple nodes is found to be untrustworthy, then it is thrown out and the most recent generally agreed upon information is searched for.

While the most common use of the Merkle tree to check for deviations in files and basic data structures whenever needed, people are now starting to use Merkle trees to check dissimilarities for entire databases and servers used throughout the websites of the world. All websites rely on the quickness of their servers so that consumers all over the world are able to connect and use it without any hassle. If a database happens to get tampered with in any way the hashes will change and the Merkle tree will be able to detect any of the inconsistencies in the server. This will stop any potential threats from taking over the retailer's site before it is too late and before any changes have gone too far.

Merkle trees are used mostly for their harmonization of all the data that they are keeping track of. This helps blockchain keep track of inconsistencies and anything else that is trying to mess with their system. With the two of them working together they will provide the best protection against any threats that happen to head in their direction.

Nonfinancial uses for blockchain

Timestamp: When using a decentralized database, it can quickly become difficult to accurately determine who did what, and when they did it. The fact that every block is automatically time stamped removes this question from the table entirely as the timestamp is created when the block is and cannot be changed at a later date.

Cloud storage: While there are not yet any public services available that offer cloud storage via blockchain, all the major names in the space are currently considering the possibilities. With a blockchain setup it could conceivably become much easier to transfer data over long distances, though the issue of storage size is still one that needs to be considered.

Licensing: This is what the Russian Federation is hoping to use blockchain 2.0 and its smart contract processes for as it could easily streamline the process of accessing and paying for digital content. The first steps towards this future can be seen within the realm of digital content, which already can connect to a bank account and deduct a set amount each time the content is used.

Social media: Perhaps one of the biggest disruptions to existing processes will come in the form of how blockchain has the potential to change social media. Leaders in this space are currently working on creating personal blockchains for individuals that provide a complete account of everything that they have ever done online as well as all the experiences that they have documented in one way or another. With the click of a button it would then be possible to literally learn everything about another person.

Public systems: Currently a majority of existing blockchains that are in wide use are those of a public nature. This means that anyone can look at or create blocks more or less whenever they choose. The natural checks that a blockchain has in place to prevent abuse in this environment make it ideal for far more than just the financial blockchains such as Ethereum or bitcoin that currently use it. The nature of the blockchain is that anyone who interacts with it agrees to play by its rules, something that will be extremely useful in many instances in the near future.

Private systems: Private blockchains have all of the security of public blockchains plus the added benefit of having a guiding hand and central authority that can ensure that things don't spin out of control in ways that are counterproductive to the goal that was stated at the creation of the blockchain. It doesn't matter what the blockchain is being used to hold, the fact that it contains multiple fail safes and levels of encryption, as well as automatically backs up its data across numerous nodes make it useful to anyone who is looking for an extremely reliable way to store important information.

Chapter 3: Deciding if Blockchain is Right for You

If you like what you have heard so far, then you are likely interested in experimenting a little with blockchain as a way of determining if it is the right course of action for you and your company. The most common reasons that people typically consider experimenting with blockchain is an ongoing desire to experiment with new technologies, a need for blockchain's timestamp technology or an interest in the many ways blockchain can safeguard existing data. It is important to look before you leap, however, and consider the following to see if blockchain is really for you.

***Know who is going to be looking at
your data****: In most traditional centralized
databases, anyone with access to the database
has their activities stored in case they need to
be reviewed later. If you have a need for many
individuals to look at your data on a regular
basis, but don't actually want to give any of
them write access then a blockchain may
streamline this process by providing read only
access in addition to a log in a more traditional
sense when required.

***Understand what your needs are
regarding writable data****: Traditional
centralized databases tend to be protected with
a standard mix of usernames and passwords
combined with disparate access levels.
Additional security measures can then be
taken to ensure that the highest-level data

remains secure against intrusion. This still pales in comparison to the digital signature a block in a blockchain comes with which always makes it clear who created what blocks and the time and date that they did so.

Essentially, this ensures that each transaction has been completed to the full knowledge of the creator who then has to confirm and sign the transaction assuming they are not adding the information directly from a node and are instead using a connected terminal. This signature is then itself confirmed by the person in charge of verifying the transaction before the block can be successfully added to an existing chain. What' s more, even if username/password identification is not required for users to gain access, something that is not recommended, the blockchain will still log the IP address of the user who created it.

Consider how you will need to alter the data that you add to the blockchain: When it comes to altering existing data in the blockchain, the process is more time consuming than with a traditional centralized database as you would be required to change the data across all nodes at once in order for the changes to not be considered aberrations and actually stick in the blockchain core. Compared to a centralized database where all you need to alter database data is the right level of clearance, this process is extremely cumbersome.

How concerned are you about data backups: When it comes to traditional centralized databases, baking up files is always going to contain a small amount of risk as you never know if the backup is going to be corrupted, or contains the right version of the data or if a disaster is going to come along and render all of the information unusable. This is not the case with blockchain, however, as the fact that it automatically updates across all the nodes in the system means that not only will making backups become something you don't need to worry about, it will be something you won't ever even need as all of your data will be ready and waiting for you across all the nodes in the network as soon as the new data is uploaded and the node in question logs back online. Depending on how much data you are backing up, and how frequently you are going to need to access it once it is in the system, the costs of running a distributed blockchain database could conceivably be cheaper than more traditional storage options.

Consider the legal ramifications: Data in a blockchain travels between nodes with relatively little consideration as to the space between those nodes. As such, if you are dealing with data that is required to remain within specific geographic areas then you are going to need to keep this fact in mind when setting up your blockchain. Simply put, if you have these types of concerns then your only option is to ensure your nodes remain in the geographic space as well.

Interconnectivity options: If your business requires exchanging databases worth of information with other individuals for a short period of time then you will likely find blockchain a welcome change as it allows you to easily connect multiple blockchains together for a predetermined period of time to allow interoperability like no other. If you create this type of interaction it is important to always take the appropriate precautions to ensure the other party can look but only touch when appropriate.

The nature of your data: Before you move forward with your blockchain database plan, it is important to ensure that the type of data you plan on storing in it is going to play well with the system. Ideally the best type of data to store in individual blocks is going to be relatively simple and fairly small as sending blocks full of gigs of data across distant nodes is a cumbersome experience that you will surly start regretting almost as soon as you begin. Unless some nature of blockchain file management balances out the trouble, larger files are likely best left to more traditional databases until Internet infrastructure improves.

The amount of data you will be validating: The biggest cost to running a decentralized database is the cost that goes into validating each and every transaction that takes place at any of the nodes in questions. To get an idea of how much this upkeep is going to cost, consider the amount of data that you are going to hold in each block and how many transactions you will ultimately need to validate each month. The lower either of these numbers, the less you will have to pay for these costs but they will still need to be paid, either by a person whose job it is to do so or by the community in exchange for some type of compensation for their time and literal energy costs.

The ultimate costs to you will eventually be determined by how popular the blockchain ends up being and how much usage it sees on a daily basis. If you run a public blockchain then you can count on individuals who will be willing to validate in exchange for incentives. Each additional individual validating means extra costs but at the same time also ensure that your chain is less likely going to errors that remain uncorrected.

Moving forward

If making your own blockchain still makes the most sense given your current situation, the next thing that you will want to do will be determined by your plan for what blockchain can do for you. If you are looking to jump in on the ground floor of blockchain with your existing business, then what you are most likely going to want to do is consider how a combination of blockchain and smart contracts can help your company react more dynamically in the marketplace to outmaneuver your competition. Good places to start when it comes to atomization include tasks that will help you to increase your revenue while decreasing costs and improving efficiency.

Additionally, you are going to want to take the time to consider how a greater adoption of blockchain technology across all facets of society is going to disrupt the status quo of the business that you are in and work to future proof your business plan to minimize its effects. Doing so will not only help you get a jump on emerging trends in your marketplace but also improve your competitive standing in the eyes of other business owners in your market. Remember, the earlier that you can determine what is coming next, the longer you have to prepare for it properly.

If, however, you find yourself with a great startup idea that you are hoping to strap to the back of blockchain in a bid for future relevancy then the first thing that you will need to do is ensure that you get as much hands-on experience with blockchain as you can in a public setting so that you become more familiar with it than your future competition will be when it finally does go main stream. On that topic, you will also want to get involved anywhere you can in an effort to ensure that the mainstream acceptance of blockchain occurs as quickly as possible.

As public blockchains catch more and more people's attention, they will slowly but surely become the natural choice when it comes to solving the types of problems that smart contracts are perfect for. The same goes for your future life changing project, the best way to ensure that it ultimately actually sees the light of day is by figuring out what problem you are planning on solving and then envisioning as many different ways to solve that problem using blockchain and smart contracts as you possibly can. Each new path you create towards solving the problem will likely iterate on the previous version a little, then a little more until it eventually is at a point where you can actually release it on the world.

Finally, if you are sure that blockchain is going to lead to something big, you just aren't sure where you fit in, then your best course of action is going to be finding the resources you need to accurately determine your next move. Just because so many people are already willing to jump blindly into the complicated waters that are blockchain doesn't mean you have to as well; remember, forewarned is forearmed. Much of blockchain's future has yet to be written, there is one thing that's clear, however, it's not going away which means you are going to need to figure out how you can use it to your advantage if you want to make it in a post blockchain world.

While planning for the future is important, so is remaining realistic about what it is going to entail. What this means is that while you can be certain innovations in the blockchain space are going to continue apace, the truth of the matter is that a majority of these are going to then fall off the map completely leaving a few new faces mixed in among the old guard who managed to pivot enough to remain relevant in the new paradigm that blockchain created. Furthermore, it will then be a safe bet that the newer business will hold the older businesses in check until they themselves become big enough that fighting the establishment no longer makes sense and the cycle repeats itself indefinitely. There are going to be two success stories when everything is said and done, you just need to know what side you are going to be on.

Chapter 4: Potential Deal Breakers

Costs*:* While there is plenty about blockchain technology to be interested in, these points of interest do in no way include being easy to operate nor being cheap to run. What's more, these are not issues that can be easily mitigated, as it is the very distributed nature of the network that is responsible for both its biggest benefits and greatest weaknesses. Each node that is created adds to the security of the network and its overall costs in equal measure; what's more, the costs are going to multiply at close to a one to one ratio as the costs will be more or less the same for setting up one node as they will be for setting up ten, with no price break for bulk along the way.

The simple fact that costs do not scale with demand makes setting up a blockchain database a nonstarter for many companies, specifically when a centralized database is already in place. While exact costs are always going to vary, a good baseline for consideration is the fact that it requires enough energy to power the average American home for 36 hours just to confirm a single bitcoin transaction. While the bitcoin blockchain is quite expansive at this point, the cost is only going to continue increasing, something to keep in mind when creating your own blockchain as well.

Prevents data mining: While consumers might consider the fact that data is encrypted to be yet another feather in bitcoins cap, marketers and major corporations certainly don't agree. This level of anonymization makes impossible for them to track the habits of individual user with currently existing technology. Again, this might sound great on the surface, but if blockchain is ever going to gain mainstream acceptance then these groups need to be on the bandwagon, not in its way.

Complicated nature: While the individual user interactions that one might have with a specific blockchain are often quite simplistic, the truth of the matter is that maintaining a blockchain can be a complicated and time consuming process, simply because of its distributed nature. As such, if you are planning on changing from a centralized to non-centralized database you need to be able to account for not just the extra time this will require but also the additional costs as well.

What's more, it is important to keep in mind that a blockchain is quite a bit more complicated than a traditional database; as such, if you are only looking for more security, and not much else, there are likely better ways to go about acquiring it. If blockchain proponents ever hope for blockchain to cross the threshold into mass acceptance, then the process of creating and maintaining them is going to need to be streamlined to a significant degree.

Ease to manipulate for the right person: While the complicated and taxing computational power required to create new blocks makes it functionally impossible to generate a profit from manipulating blockchains, and thus ensures its more or less total security, this does not mean it is impossible to do so for someone who was properly motivated. If the need were great enough it is logical to assume that a person, or group of people, would come up with the resources required to generate enough blocks to essentially rewrite the entire chain to the specifications of their choosing. Again, this is functionally impossible at the end of 2016, but when blockchain catches on in a big way then this could conceivably no longer be the case.

It supports big business: While blockchain technology has so far been gaining acceptance among what are essentially a fringe minority, the fact of the matter is that major corporations have the most to gain from using this technology. They are the ones that have the massive infrastructure to require and the resources to fund the shift from centralized to decentralized servers. Every new technology ends up pushing a few new players into the limelight, and blockchain will be no different; those expecting blockchain to change the way the game is played are going to be sadly mistaken however. This isn't necessarily a mark against blockchain; it is simply something to keep in mind when blockchain is inevitably heralded as the tool that will finally free the everyman from his oppressors.

Creates a new layer of security concerns: While bitcoin miners are able to act with relative anonymity, once blockchain is put to work for major corporations and private blockchains become the norm it is logical to assume that those who are hired to verify transactions will be held to an extreme degree of security. This will certainly be required as these individuals are going to essentially have carte blanche when it comes to ensuring the system functions as intended. The amount of power that individuals in this position will hold will require an entire new level of security to monitor properly which means increased costs, at the very least.

Too efficient for trading: While many in the financial sector expect blockchain to come through and rewrite the rules for asset trading overnight, the reality is that those who trade in assets actually like the current pace of the market. The fact of the matter is that real time settlements are different from same day settlements because they allow the buyer to receive their shares in an extremely quick manner. This sounds good in theory, except for the fact that these shares are frequently at work for those who currently hold them and letting them go immediately would cause far more trouble than it would prevent.

Think of it this way, if you and your brother are having dinner at a restaurant and your brother pays the bill, then the next time you go out to eat with your brother you pay the bill, then you are going to be functionally even despite the fact that the total of the two meals was for differing amounts. This same principal applies to day traders who do not want to have to settle up after every single transaction, instead preferring to deal in lump sums at the end of the day. Furthermore, many countries have been dealing in same-day exchanges for years, and there are even certain markets where you can make same-day exchanges in the US as well. What it comes down to is that the way it is, is simply the way it is and that is unlikely to change anytime soon.

It needs to gain popularity at the right speed: While the idea of blockchain spreading like wildfire and gaining mainstream usage within 12 months might sound good in theory, the reality is that a slow and steady increase in mainstream usage is going to be more beneficial in the long term. This is the case because the version of blockchain that is ultimately going to stick around the longest is the one that catches on with the mainstream and there are still bugs to be worked out before that happens. If the technology catches on before it is ready, then any existing problems become much harder to fix as they are now hardwired into what most people think of as the only version of blockchain that has ever existed.

As such, a growth and acceptance rate that continues to move along at a slow, reliable pace is likely to turn out the best results as it will give blockchain programmers the time they need to get all of the hitches out before things really take off. This is a moment where blockchain's decentralized nature works against it instead of for it as a centralized authority could easily step in and enforce an update no matter how widespread previous versions of the software may be. If you need proof that this is the case, consider how long copies of Windows XP remained in the wild versus how quickly people update to a new phone operating system once it is made available.

The blockchain technology is going to be at a crossroads soon, and if things do not happen in the appropriate way, then there is a very real possibility that it may fall by the wayside. While this might seem a big overdramatic, the very same thing once almost happened to the Internet. In that case, it was TCP/IP, which would have been easy to improve upon at the time if anyone had been in charge to focus existing programmers on the problem. While workarounds were found eventually that bypassed their importance, it could have been easily fixed early on if someone had been in charge and spent a minute thinking about the core building blocks that makes the internet work. The best-case scenario for blockchain then is to hold on as a viable alternative to traditional databases long enough for a major piece of technology to come along and push it into the limelight once and for all.

Chapter 5: Blockchain Implementation Mistakes to Avoid

While there are certainly plenty of reasons to implement your own blockchain system, the previous chapter has proven that it isn't for everyone, at least not in its current configuration. Even if you are convinced that blockchain is the solution that you have been waiting for, there is still plenty that can go wrong when it comes to implementing the new database in a way that ensures things proceed as smoothly as possible. Consider the following common mistakes that people often make once they go ahead and take the plunge to ensure that you don't end up following too closely in their footsteps.

Anticipating blockchain to be a type of cure-all: There is plenty of hype these days regarding just what exactly a blockchain database can do for you, so you can be forgiven for letting your expectations get a little carried away. There are still limits, however, and while it can be used in a wide variety of scenarios, only so many of those will ultimately cause it to behave differently than a more traditional database. This is why it is important to consider exactly what you are going to be doing with your blockchain database before setting it up, not after.

This is especially important when it comes to the amount of data that you are going to be storing in your database as the sum total of all of it is going to be copied into every node that you set up out of the gate as well as down the line. While an extra gigabyte of data here or there might not seem like much on paper, you will certainly feel it when it comes to the increase in time you will have to endure every time you want to call up something that is not directly accessible from your location. Remember, bitcoins blockchain is only around 60 gigs total. The lesson here is that the most effective blockchain databases are those that may need to store large amounts of data but only need to access portions of it at any given time.

Another important fact to consider when it comes to blockchain databases is that despite the fact that they natural include fail safes against user error, they are no more immune to it than a traditional centralized database might be. In fact, they might be more prone to error from employees that are not properly trained as most of the time individual blocks can only be identified via their hash identifier, which is far from clear to the uninitiated. While this will become less of an issue once blockchain technology becomes more common place, it is important to remember that for now there is more to getting a blockchain database up and running smoothing than starting the first node and having at it.

Underestimating blockchain's complexity: When it comes to ensuring that a blockchain transition is actually followed through to completion, one of the most important things you will need is a road map of just what needs to happen, and to create an accurate map you need to know how to take advantage of blockchain to its full potential. What this means is that this book is a great first step, but it is only that, and if you truly want to make implementing a blockchain database worth the increased cost then there is going to be more to learn.

To ensure you are pointed in the right direction it is important that you go into the endeavor with a clear understanding of what the primary use of the database is going to be along with its secondary and tertiary responsibilities might entail. This then will allow you to consider the various blockchain creation tools at your disposal that will make the creation process as manageable as possible. Just because blockchain isn't yet a technology that is on the lips of the mainstream doesn't mean that the market isn't already crowded with creation software tools that came make things flow much more smoothly from start to finish. Rushing through this step could set you on a course for failure that may be difficult to recover from, don't risk it and do your research.

Underestimating the time it will take: It is important to be sure to schedule enough time to get your decentralized database up and running as rushing or being impatient will only lead to additional difficulties further down the line. The steps to the process, as discussed in chapter 6, are very precise and not following things to the letter or failing to test your creation before letting it go live is a good way to ensure you will only have to repeat the process a second time. As such, you will find that providing yourself with a bit of a padded timeframe will only help your cause, especially if you know you are going to need to get buy-in from multiple sources before you can actually get to work.

Relying too heavily on the built-in fail safes: Much has been made about the vigorous nature of blockchain's security, so you may be forgiven for thinking that gives you a free pass to hand out invitations to the blockchain, especially on a private variation where things are innately more controlled. The truth of the matter is that even if they don't mean too, giving people access to the blockchain who have not been properly trained first, is a great way to cause a fledgling blockchain to buckle under the weight of too much inaccurate information collected before it has enough reliable data to weed out the troublemakers. The security around the core of your blockchain, essentially its beating heart, should be kept under only the strictest security and stored someplace that will always be readily available. Remember, if you lose access to the key then you lose control of the blockchain, it is as simple as that.

Overestimating smart contracts: A smart contract is a type of code that can be added to a blockchain to allow it to do more than simply keep track of existing information; it allows it to act on that information once certain specifications are met.

The smart contract can be triggered by an authorized event and can process anything stored in it like a traditional block in the chain; as such, if money were supposed to move between accounts once a certain amount is reached, then this would happen automatically. If, for some reason, someone tries to change a transaction on the blockchain any others involved in the transaction will be able to prevent it if needed. Regardless, the data will be able to continue even if the system fails for one person in the party.

The idea behind the smart contract is that it can enforce the obligation that is in a traditional contract. Despite the name, however, smart contracts and traditional contracts actually have little in common. The most important fact that distinguishes a smart contract from a traditional contract is the fact that it is not legally enforceable in the same way that a more traditional contract is. To illustrate, a smart contract could be set up to guarantee your car payment is made each month, and even shut down your engine if your car was internet-enabled were the payments not made, but it could not legally force you to make those payments if you didn't want to.

Instead, you will likely find smart contracts to be most useful when it comes to automating specific processes that are outlined in more traditional contracts. Virtually any if/then statement can be made into a smart contract as long as the qualifiers are going to exist in a blockchain for it to verify. It is also worth noting that smart contracts are different than what are known as Ricardian contracts as well. A Ricardian contract determines liability, a smart contact will only activate after liability has been determined. Smart contracts have no notion of liability, they are essentially a switch that can be set to on or off.

Furthermore, despite the name, smart contracts aren't actually all that smart. In fact, while they can be programed in numerous different ways, there is little actually going on in their code except a simple trigger that can cause something to happen given the right stimuli. They are literally nothing more than a few lines of code without the right set of external events happening in their favor. The limits that they do have are decreasing, however, which means that as blockchains become more prevalent the number of functions a smart contract will perform is only going to increase. Despite their relatively limited use, the variety of situations where they can come in handy is already staggering, to say nothing of where it is likely to be in the next several years. Soon, any routine action that has clear indicators surrounding it will realistically be able to be operated by blockchain control as long as it is connected to the Internet.

Last but not least, you need to be aware that smart contracts live within blocks; they don't create blocks of their own. Remember, blockchain is an example of a distributed database in action while a smart contract is distributed computing in action.

Chapter 6: Creating Your Own Smart Contracts

If, after weighing your options, you are still interested in proceeding apace with your very own blockchain with the possibility of including your own smart contracts as well, then you are going to want to start off by working with the platform that Ethereum has created. As previously noted, Ethereum practically wrote the book when it comes to blockchain 2.0 and is still considered the leader in that part of the space. Much like bitcoin, Ethereum is a crypto currency, which, unlike bitcoin, is primarily focused on providing a way for those seeking services to pay for those services via non-traditional means. It is also used to run a number of other applications that have been created on its platform. The currency of Ethereum is ether and 1 ether is worth about $7.50 in December 2016.

One of the most unique aspects of Ethereum is its ability to host applications that are decentralized as well as databases. Each application can then link directly to the blockchain and connect to any existing smart contracts without having to log into an actual node to do so. This means that you do not technically need to run your own node to take advantage of all that Ethereum has to offer, though it is recommended as it will be great practice for what is to come and will also make testing smart contracts much less of a hassle.

Furthermore, if you plan on creating your own smart contracts then it is recommended that you do so in the programming language known as Solidity, which is related to JavaScript. When doing so, it is also recommended that you download LLL, which was created from Lisp, and always use the extensions .sol or .se. Solidity should immediately feel familiar to anyone who has previously used either Python or Serpent.

When it comes time to compile contracts that you have created, the best way to do so is with the C++ Solc Compiler. If you would instead prefer a browser-based alternative, then Cosmo is typically considered the best option available today. The remainder of this walkthrough will assume that you proceeded via the Solc complier path, though the same instructions should typically apply to Cosmo. Once you have finished compiling the contract, the next step will be to download the Web3.ja API, which will allow you to interact with your smart contracts via the Ethereum application.

Distributed application frameworks

If the thought of building your own framework is enough to send you running in the opposite direction, then you are in luck as there are plenty of free options floating around online that were created with the goal of improving the viability of the marketplace as a whole.

Embark/Truffle: Truffle is great for those who are looking to automate as much of the process as possible when it comes to general programming steps that will always need to be performed no matter what. With these steps out of the way you will then have more time to create the best code that you can by focusing on the deployment, testing and compiling of changes, as they are needed. Embark then helps further streamline the testing and building processes even more.

Meteor: When it comes to stacks that are useful for working with blockchain conventional wisdom says that Meteor with it web3.js offering is the best web application framework around at the moment. Meteor is likely going to become even more important in the coming days as it was discussed repeatedly at the Ethereum Development conference held in November of 2016.

APIs: When it comes to the APIs that are used by the majority of all Ethereum based applications the majority of them come from BlockApps.net. This is where you can find the API that allows you to mimic a traditional Ethereum node so you can interact with your smart contracts on the go. MetaMask is another popular API that will give you access to the full suite of Ethereum tools from any standard web browser. Last but not least, Light Wallet is the most in-depth API currently available and is the one most preferred by professional developers.

Installing Geth

In order to create your very own blockchain the first thing that you are going to want to do is install the primary interface for all Ethereum nodes and applications which is known as

Geth. Installing Geth is as easy as typing bash<(curlhttps://install-geth.ethereum.org) into your command line. With that, you will be given a prompt asking if you wish to install Geth, and if so, choose the current version of the Ethereum CLL and your current operating system.

After the installation has finished, you will then be able to interact with the Geth interface in much the same way you would a JavaScript environment while still having full use of the console as well. Any use you make of the console will be tracked between uses to make it easy to always pick up where you left off.

With everything ready to go, the next thing that you will need to do is to open the terminal tool to gain access to the Geth console. Once the program has launched you will want to keep an eye out for a simple > which will be your notification that everything is working properly. When you wish to quit all that is required is to type "exit" followed by the ENTER key. When working in Geth you have the means to redirect as well as log console outputs using the command gethconsole2>>geth.log. You may also find this log via the command tailfgeth.log.

Testing the smart contract

When you create your smart contract, it is important that all of your if/then statements are written properly as you have no leeway when it comes to having the smart contract determine if a specific event has come to pass. The easiest way to test this sort of thing is via

Truffle, which can automatically create the type of framework for promises that are required for both JavaScript as well as Web3.js.

Time transaction test: When it comes to creating smart contract promises it is important that you make them as simple as possible as no blockchain verification can be completed in less than 10 seconds, and even then that is only under optimal testing conditions. As such, the more promises that need to be cross-referenced the slower it is going to be.

When you get ready to actually test the contract you will want to start by relabeling the .js file so that it reads conference.js, when you do this it is important to reroute any other references as well. With this done, all that is left for you to do is open Truffle and run the test for the root directory that houses the contract.

To test the contract properly you are going to also want to open Solidity, Pip and Solc, taking special care to keep the test library and the main library separate just to be safe. You will then need to open the console window and generate a new client node before starting Truffle via the truffle deploy command and keep contracts to the standard init. Doing so will tell the program to note any errors in the code so you don't need to track them down yourself. During this process, it is considered good practice to test the compilation as well, which can also be done via Truffle to prevent the compilation process from giving you errors at the last minute.

Finishing the smart contract

After you have created the smart contract of your dreams in Solidity, you are going to want to compile it via the Solc compiler as previously mentioned. Once this has finished, you will be ready to deploy by signing a digital signature marking you as the content creator and also paying an ether fee to get things up and running. With this out of the way you will be given a unique URL that links to the contract and the ABI of the contract, which can interact, with the API of your choice. Checking on your contract in general is free, though there will likely be other options available that you can access for an additional ether fee.

When creating a smart contract, it is important to always be sure to include a variable that will allow you to shut down the smart contract via what is known as contract suicide. You never know when you might want to take the contract out of commission and without including this feature in the creation of the contract you will find it quite difficult to go back and do so later on. Do yourself a favor and always include this option to prevent a scenario where money transfers from one account but fails to transfer to the other, leaving your funds in limbo, potentially forever unless you get everything right.

Deploying the smart contract

Once the contract is ready to go, it can be deployed via Truffle from the console via the command "truffle init" followed by the name of the new directory you wish to create. With this done you will then be able to find the contract you are looking for by looking for its name followed by the extension .sol. After you find the contract you will want to open the config file for app.json before adding the new contract in the space for contract names. With this done all that is left to do is open an Ethereum node in a separate console window and input the command to run the tesrpc. Assuming everything works properly you can then deploy from Truffle using the deploy option in the root directory.

Notes on variables

First and foremost, smart contract variables will always be listed in the same order starting with address, which is the location of your Ethereum wallet, which is where any funds may ultimately be deposited. After address the next variable will be uinit, which stands for unsigned integer, nearly all of the time this variable will remain at 256. The next variable will be set to public or private. Typically private is going to be the correct choice unless the smart contract needs access to details that it cannot find in the blockchain in order to activate properly.

Conclusion

Thank for making it through to the end of *Blockchain: The Database Revolution That Will Change the World! I* hope that you found it informative and that you can build on this knowledge to achieve your goals with blockchain, whatever it is that they may be. Just because you've finished this book doesn't mean there is nothing left to learn on the topic, expanding your horizons is the only way to find the mastery you seek.

Currently, blockchains are largely used for their data transmission abilities, primarily in the financial sector. This is all about to change, and sooner than many might expect, and if you want to get in on the ground floor then you are going to want to be aware of as many of these possibilities as possible. Despite the fact that real world examples of smart contracts are relatively few and far between, more and more applications are being discovered every day. Currently many smart contracts are in the hands of those already in power, automatic deductions from your checking account are a good example, as the bank is ultimately in complete control over what happens to your money. Future smart contracts are going to return the power to the people, but only the technology develops in the right way, something you could quite possibly have a hand in.

Blockchain and smart contract implementation knows virtually no limits and the time to start searching for them is now. If you aren't sure about which direction you want to move in, fear not, there are plenty to choose from and you are still ahead of the curve so there is little rush. Take your time and find the niche that speaks to you, remember, mastery of blockchain is a marathon, not a sprint, slow and steady wins the race. Take you time to consider all of your possible options and the right way for you to move forward with blockchain will eventually reveal itself, you can be sure it is worth the wait.

Finally, if you found this book useful in anyway, a review on Amazon is always appreciated!

About the Author

Jake Whitley reached No.1 Best Seller in his category for his first book, *"Passive Income: Step-by-Step How To Turn The Top 6 Online Strategies into a Single Money Making Machine"*

He has been actively involved with SEO and Internet Marketing since 2008. Before creating his own 'online business' Jake spent four years working as a SEO consultant and specialist at one of the UK's leading search engine optimization agencies. Since branching out on his own he has become well known in his community for brand building and product creation. His passion has become creating truly passive streams of income by utilizing the latest technology and social media.